D0386497

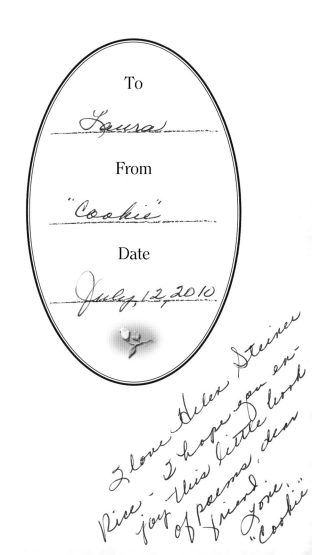

To

Laura

From

"Cookie"

Date

July, 12 2010

I love Helen Steiner
Rice - I hope you en-
joy this little book
of poems, dear
friend.
Love,
"Cookie"

God's Love for You

Copyright © 2006 by the Helen Steiner Rice Foundation.
All rights reserved. Poems selected from publications
compiled by Virginia J. Ruehlmann.

© 2006 Christian Art Gifts, RSA
        Christian Art Gifts Inc., IL, USA

Artwork copyright © 2006 by Cathi Freund, licensed by
Suzanne Cruise

Designed by Christian Art Gifts

Scripture taken from the *Holy Bible*, New International
Version®. NIV®. Copyright © 1973, 1978, 1984 by Inter-
national Bible Society. Used by permission of Zondervan
Publishing House. All rights reserved.

Printed in China

ISBN 1-86920-356-9

© All rights reserved. No part of this book may be
reproduced in any form without permission in writing
from the publisher, except in the case of brief quotations
embodied in critical articles or reviews.

06 07 08 09 10 11 12 13 14 15 – 10 9 8 7 6 5 4 3 2

God's Love for You

A Helen Steiner Rice® Collection

Artwork by Cathi Freund

christian art gifts®

Contents

The comfort and sweetness of peace

After the clouds, the sunshine,
after the winter, the spring,
after the shower, the rainbow,
for life is a changeable thing.

After the night, the morning,
bidding all darkness cease,
after life's cares and sorrows,
the comfort and sweetness of peace.

Blessings in everything

Blessings come in many guises
that God alone in love devises,
and sickness
which we dread so much
can bring a very healing touch.
For often on the wings of pain
the peace we sought before in vain
will come to us with sweet surprise
for God is merciful and wise,
and through long hours of tribulation
God gives us time for meditation,
and no sickness
can be counted a loss
that teaches us to bear our cross.

My flesh and my heart
may fail, but God is
the strength of my heart
and my portion forever.

PSALM 73:26

Dark shadows

Sickness and sorrow
come to us all,
but through it we grow
and learn to stand tall.

And the more we endure
with patience and grace
the stronger we grow
and the more we can face.

And the more we can face,
the greater our love,
and with love in our hearts
we are more conscious of
the pain and the sorrow
in lives everywhere,
so it is through trouble
that we learn how to share.

The LORD
is close to the brokenhearted
and saves those
who are crushed in spirit.
PSALM 34:18

Look for the best

It's easy to grow downhearted
when nothing goes your way,
it's easy to be discouraged
when you have a troublesome day,
but trouble is only a challenge
to spur you on to achieve
the best that God has to offer
if you have the faith to believe!

The answer

In the tiny petal
of a tiny flower
that grew from a tiny pod ...

Is the miracle
and the mystery
of all creation and God!

Finding faith in a flower

Sometimes when faith is running low
and I cannot fathom
why things are so ...
I walk alone among the flowers I grow
and learn the answers
to all I would know.

For among my flowers
I have come to see
life's miracle and its mystery ...
And standing in silence and reverie
my faith comes flooding back to me!

All nature proclaims eternal life

Flowers sleeping 'neath the snow,
awakening when the Spring winds blow;
leafless trees so bare before,
gowned in lacy green once more.

Hard, unyielding, frozen sod
now softly carpeted by God;
still streams melting in the Spring
rippling over rocks that sing;
barren, windswept, lonely hills
turning gold with daffodils ...

These miracles are all around
within our sight and touch and sound,
as true and wonderful today
as when the stone was rolled away,
proclaiming to all doubting men
that in God all things live again.

Praise the LORD, O my soul, and forget not all His benefits — who forgives all your sins and heals all your diseases, who redeems your life from the pit and crowns you with love and compassion, who satisfies your desires with good things so that your youth is renewed like the eagle's.

PSALM 103:2-5

Let your life
become a prayer

Sometimes when a light
goes out of our life
and we are left
in darkness
and do not know
which way to go,
we must put our hand
into the hand of God
and ask Him to lead us.

And if we let our life
become a prayer
until we are strong enough
to stand under the weight
of our own thoughts again,
somehow even the most difficult
hours are bearable.

Beyond the clouds

Most of the battles
of life are won
by looking
beyond the clouds
to the sun,
and having the patience
to wait for the day
when the sun comes out
and the clouds float away!

A prayer
for healing

I wish I knew some magic words to say
to take your troubles all away,
but at times like this we realize
that God, who is both kind and wise,
can do what none of us can do,
and that's to heal and comfort you.
So I commend you to His care,
and may He hear your smallest prayer
and grant returning health to you
as only He alone can do.

He sent forth His word
and healed them.

PSALM 107:20

Those who *hope* in the *Lord*
will renew their *strength.*
They will *soar on wings*
like *eagles;* they will *run*
and not grow *weary,*
they will
walk
and not be
faint.

ISAIAH 40:31

On the wings
of prayer

On the wings of prayer
our burdens take flight
and our load of care
becomes bearably light
and our heavy hearts
are lifted above
to be healed by the balm
of God's wonderful love.

And the tears in our eyes
are dried by the hands
of a loving Father
who understands
all of our problems,
our fears and despair
when we take them to Him
on the wings of prayer.

God bless you
and keep you

There are many things in life
that we cannot understand,
but we must trust God's judgment
and be guided by His hand,
and all who have God's blessing
can rest safely in His care,
for He promises safe passage
on the wings of faith and prayer.

God's tender care

When trouble comes,
as it does to us all
God is so great
and we are so small -
but there is nothing
that we need know
if we have faith
that wherever we go
God will be waiting
to help us bear
our pain and sorrow,
our suffering and care.
For no pain or suffering
is ever too much
to yield itself
to God's merciful touch!

What more
can you ask

God's love endureth forever –
what a wonderful thing to know
when the tides of life run against you
and your spirit is downcast and low.

God's kindness is ever around you,
always ready to freely impart
strength to your faltering spirit
cheer to your lonely heart.

God's presence is ever beside you,
as near as the reach of your hand,
you have but to tell Him your troubles –
there is nothing He won't understand.

And knowing God's love is unfailing,
and His mercy unending and great,
you have but to trust in His promise -
God comes not too soon or too late.

So wait with a heart that is patient
for the goodness of God to prevail,
for never do prayers go unanswered,
and His mercy and love never fail.

Peace and calm in the 23rd Psalm

With the Lord as your Shepherd
you have all that you need,
for, if you follow in His footsteps
wherever He may lead,
He will guard and guide and keep you
in His loving, watchful care,
and when traveling in dark valleys,
your Shepherd will be there.
His goodness is unfailing,
His kindness knows no end,
for the Lord is the Good Shepherd
on whom you can depend ...
So, when your heart is troubled,
you'll find quiet, peace and calm
if you'll open up the Bible
and just read this treasured Psalm.

Surely goodness and love will follow
me all the days of my life,
and I will dwell in
the house of the LORD forever.

PSALM 23:6

Comfort

Although it sometimes seems to us
our prayers have not been heard,
God always knows our every need
without a single word.

And He will not forsake us
even though the way seems steep,
for always He is near to us,
a tender watch to keep.

And in good time, He'll answer us,
and in His love He'll send
greater things than we have asked
and blessings without end.

So though we do not understand
why trouble comes to man,
can we not be contented
just to know that it's God's plan.

When troubles come

When troubles come
and things go wrong,
and days are cheerless
and nights are long,
we find it so easy to give in to despair
by magnifying the burdens we bear.
We add to our worries
by refusing to try
to look for the rainbow
in an overcast sky -
and the blessing God sent
is a darkened disguise
our troubled hearts fail to recognize,
not knowing God sent it
not to distress us,
but to strengthen our faith and redeem
and bless us.

"Peace I leave with you;
My peace I give you.
I do not give to you
as the world gives.
Do not let your hearts be troubled
and do not be afraid."

JOHN 14:27

God is beside you

Our Father in heaven
always knows what is best,
and if you trust in His wisdom,
your life will be blessed ...

For always remember that,
whatever betide you,
you are never alone,
for God is beside you.

The salvation of the righteous comes
from the LORD;
He is their stronghold
in time of trouble.

PSALM 37:39

Our refuge and our strength

The Lord is our salvation
and our strength in every fight,
Our Redeemer and Protector,
our eternal guiding light ...

He has promised to sustain us,
He's our refuge from all harms,
and He holds us all securely
in His everlasting arms!

Secure in His love

Just close your eyes
and open your heart
and feel your worries
and cares depart ...
Just yield yourself
to the Father above
and let Him hold you
secure in His love.

For He hears every prayer
and answers each one
when we pray in His name,
"Thy will be done,"
and the burdens that seemed
too heavy to bear
are lifted away
on the wings of a prayer.

For the eyes of the

and His ears are

Lord are on the righteous attentive to their prayer.

1 PETER 3:12

New strength

We all have those days
that are dismal and dreary
and we feel sort of blue
and lonely and weary,
but we have to admit
that life is worth living
and God gives us reasons
for daily thanksgiving ...

For each trial we suffer
and every shed tear
just gives us new strength
to persevere
as we climb the steep hills
along life's way
that lead us at last
to that wonderful day
where the cross we have carried
becomes a crown
and at last we can lay
our burden down!

This too will
pass away

If I can endure for this minute
whatever is happening to me,
no matter how heavy my heart is
or how dark the moment may be ...

If I can remain calm and quiet
with all my world crashing about me,
secure in the knowledge God loves me
when everyone else seems to doubt me ...

If I can but keep on believing
what I know in my heart to be true,
that darkness will fade with the morning
and that this will pass away, too ...

Then nothing in life can defeat me
for as long as this knowledge remains
I can suffer whatever is happening
for I know God will break all the chains
that are binding me tight in the darkness
and trying to fill me with fear -
for there is no night without dawning
and I know that my morning is near.

Ideals are like stars

Remember that ideals
are like stars up in the sky,
you can never really reach them,
hanging in the heavens high ...

But like the mighty mariner
who sailed the storm-tossed sea,
and used the stars
to chart his course
with skill and certainty,
you too can chart your course in life
with high ideals and live,
for high ideals are like the stars
that light the sky above ...

You cannot ever reach them,
but lift your heart up high
and your life will be as shining
as the stars up in the sky.

Cheerful thoughts

Cheerful thoughts like sunbeams
lighten up the darkest fears
for when the heart is happy
there's just no time for tears ...

And when the face is smiling
it's impossible to frown
and when you are high-spirited
you cannot feel low-down ...

And since fear and dread and worry
cannot help in any way,
it's much healthier and happier
to be cheerful every day ...

For when the heart is cheerful
it cannot be filled with fear
and without fear, the way ahead
seems more distinct and clear ...

And we realize there's nothing
we need ever face alone
for our heavenly Father loves us
and our problems are His own.

The Savior's loving hand

Take the Savior's loving hand
and do not try to understand,
just let Him lead you where He will
through pastures green, by waters still,
and place yourself in His loving care
and He will gladly help you bear
whatever lies ahead of you
He will see you safely through,
no earthly pain is ever too much
if God bestows His merciful touch.

"Do not fear, for I am with you;
do not be dismayed,
for I am your God.
I will strengthen you and help you;
I will uphold you
with My righteous right hand."

ISAIAH 41:10

Go to God
in prayer

Whenever I am troubled
and lost in deep despair
I bundle all my troubles up
and go to God in prayer ...

I tell Him I am heartsick
and lost and lonely, too,
that my heart is deeply burdened
and I don't know what to do ...

But I know He stilled the tempest
and calmed the angry sea
and I humbly ask if in His love
He'll do the same for me ...

And then I just keep quiet
and think only thoughts of peace
and if I abide in stillness
my restless murmurings cease.

You, dear children,
are from God
and have overcome them,
because the One who is in you
is greater than
the one who is in the world.

1 JOHN 4:4

Praise the LORD from the heavens,
praise Him in the heights above.
Praise Him, all His angels,
praise Him, all His heavenly hosts.
Praise Him, sun and moon, praise
Him, all you shining stars.

PSALM 148:1-3

Two sides

There are always two sides,
the good and the bad,
the dark and the light,
the sad and the glad,
but in looking back over
the good and the bad
we're aware of the number
of good things we've had.

So thank God for good things
He has already done,
and be grateful to Him
for the battles you've won,
and know that the same God
who helped you before
is ready and willing
to help you once more.

So many reasons to love the Lord

Thank You, God, for little things
that come unexpectedly
to brighten up a dreary day
that dawned so dismally.

Thank You, God, for sending
a happy thought my way
to blot out my depression
on a disappointing day.

Thank You, God, for brushing
the dark clouds from my mind
and leaving only sunshine
and joy of heart behind ...

Oh, God the list is endless
of things to thank You for,
but I take them all for granted
and unconsciously ignore
that everything I think or do,
each movement that I make,
each measured, rhythmic heartbeat,
each breath of life I take
is something You have given me
for which there is no way
for me in all my smallness
to in any way repay.

God is never beyond our reach

No one ever sought the Father
and found He was not there,
and no burden is too heavy
to be lightened by a prayer.
No problem is too intricate
and no sorrow that we face
is too deep and devastating
to be softened by His grace.
No trials and tribulations
are beyond what we can bear
if we share them with our Father
and we talk to Him in prayer.

*God is our refuge
and strength,
an ever-present help
in trouble.*

PSALM 46:1

You have filled my

than when their grain

heart with greater joy
and new wine abound.

PSALM 4:7

The peace
of meditation

So we may know God better
and feel His quiet power,
let us daily keep in silence
a meditation hour.

For to understand God's greatness
and to use His gifts each day
the soul must learn to meet Him
in a meditative way.

For our Father tells His children
that if they would know His will
they must seek Him in the silence
when all is calm and still ...

For nature's greatest forces
are found in quiet things
like softly falling snowflakes
drifting down on angels' wings,
or petals dropping soundlessly
from a lovely full-blown rose,
so God comes closest to us
when our souls are in repose ...

So let us plan with prayerful care
to always allocate
a certain portion of each day
to be still and meditate ...

For when everything is quiet
and we're lost in meditation,
our soul is then preparing
for a deeper dedication
that will make it wholly possible
to quietly endure
the violent world around us –
for in God we are secure.

Safely in His care

Prayers for big and little things
fly heavenward on angels' wings -
and He who walked by the Galilee
and touched the blind
and made them see,
and cured the man who long was lame
when he but called God's holy name,
will keep you safely in His care
and when you need Him,
He'll be there!

Enfolded by love

The love of God
surrounds us
like the air we breathe
around us -
as near
as a heartbeat,
as close as a prayer,
and whenever we need Him
He'll always be there!

Someone cares

Someone cares and always will,
the world forgets,
but God loves you still.
You cannot go beyond His love
no matter what you're guilty of.

For God forgives until the end,
He is your faithful, loyal friend,
and though you try to hide your face
there is no shelter in any place
that can escape His watchful eye,
for on the earth and in the sky
He's ever present and always there
to take you in His tender care
and bind the wounds
and mend the breaks
when all the world around forsakes.

Someone cares and loves you still,
and God is the Someone
who always will.

In the morning, O LORD,
You hear my voice;
in the morning
I lay my requests before
You and wait in expectation.

PSALM 5:3

When I consider Your heavens,
the work of Your fingers,
the moon and the stars,
which You have set in place,
what is man
that You are mindful of him,
the son of man
that You care for him?
You made him a little lower than
the heavenly beings and crowned
him with glory and honor.

PSALM 8:3-5

Why should He die for such as I?

In everything both great and small
we see the hand of God in all,
and in the miracles of Spring
when everywhere in everything
His handiwork is all around
and every lovely sight and sound
proclaims the God of earth and sky,
I ask myself, "Just who am I
that God should send His only Son
that my salvation would be won
upon a cross by a sinless Man
to bring fulfillment to God's plan?"
For Jesus suffered, bled and died
that sinners might be sanctified,
and to grant God's children such as I
eternal life in that home on high.

Never forsaken

The seasons swiftly come and go
and with them comes the thought
of all the various changes
that time in flight has brought ...

But one thing never changes,
it remains the same forever,
God truly loves His children
and He will forsake them never!

Listen for God

Within the crowded city,
where life is swift and fleet
do you ever look for Jesus
upon the busy street?

Above the noise and laughter,
that is empty, cruel, and loud
do you listen for the voice of God
in the restless surging crowd?

Do you pause in meditation
upon life's thoroughfare
and offer up thanksgiving
or say a word of prayer?

Well, if you would find the Savior,
no need to search afar
for God is all around you
no matter where you are.

The heavens declare the glory of God;
the skies proclaim the work
of His hands. Day after day they
pour forth speech; night after night
they display knowledge.

PSALM 19:1-2

Sunshine and rain

No one likes to be sick
and yet we know
it takes sunshine and rain
to make flowers grow ...

And if we never were sick
and never felt pain,
we'd be like a desert
without any rain,
and who wants a life
that is barren and dry
with never a cloud
to darken the sky ...

For continuous sun
goes unrecognized
like the blessings God sends
which are often disguised,
for sometimes a sickness
that seems so distressing
is a time of renewal
and a spiritual blessing.

God's tender care

When trouble comes,
as it does to us all
God is so great
and we are so small ...

But there is nothing
that we need know
if we have faith
that wherever we go
God will be waiting
to help us bear
our pain and sorrow,
our suffering and care ...

For no pain or suffering
is ever too much
to yield itself
to God's merciful touch !

"Be still, and know that I am God."

PSALM 46:10

In God's keeping

To be in God's keeping
is surely a blessing,
for though life is often
dark and distressing,
no day is too dark
and no burden too great
that God in His love
cannot penetrate,
and to know and believe
without question or doubt
that no matter what happens
God is there to help out,
is to hold in your hand
the golden key
to peace and joy
and serenity !

Because He lives, we too shall live

In this restless world of struggle
it is very hard to find
answers to the questions
that daily come to mind.

We cannot see the future,
what's beyond is still unknown,
for the secret of God's kingdom
still belongs to Him alone.

But He granted us salvation
when His Son was crucified,
for life became immortal
because our Savior died.

We can't,
but God can

Why things happen as they do
we do not always know,
and we cannot always fathom
why our spirits sink so low.

We flounder in our dark distress,
we are wavering and unstable,
but when we're most inadequate
the Lord God's always able,
for though we are incapable,
God's powerful and great,
and there's no darkness of the mind
He cannot penetrate.

And all that is required of us
whenever things go wrong
is to trust in God implicitly
with a faith that's deep and strong,
and while He may not instantly
unravel all the strands
of all the tangled thoughts
that trouble us,
He completely understands,
and in His time, if we have faith,
He will gradually restore
the brightness to our spirit
that we've been longing for.

So remember there's no cloud too dark
for God's light to penetrate
if we keep on believing
and have faith enough to wait.

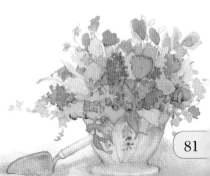

Prayers are the stairs to God

Prayers are the stairs
we must climb every day,
if we would reach God
there is no other way,
for we learn to know God
when we meet Him in prayer
and ask Him to lighten
our burden of care.

So start in the morning
and, though the way's steep,
climb ever upward
till your eyes close in sleep.

For prayers are the stairs
that lead to the Lord,
and to meet Him in prayer
is the climber's reward.

God whispering

Each time you look up in the sky
or watch the fluffy clouds drift by,
or feel the sunshine warm and bright,
or watch the dark night turn to light,
or hear a bluebird gaily sing,
or see the winter turn to spring,
or stop to pick a daffodil,
or gather violets on some hill,
or touch a leaf or see a tree,
it's all God whispering, "This is Me -
and I am faith and I am light
and in Me there shall be no night."

How great is the love
the Father has lavished on us,
that we should be called
children of God!
And that is what we are!

1 JOHN 3:1

Love: God's gift divine

Love is enduring
and patient and kind,
it judges all things
with the heart not the mind,
and love can transform
the most commonplace
into beauty and splendor
and sweetness and grace.

For love is unselfish,
giving more than it takes,
and no matter what happens
love never forsakes,
it's faithful and trusting,
and always believing,
guileless and honest
and never deceiving.

Yes, love is beyond
what man can define,
for love is immortal
and God's gift is divine!

Help yourself to happiness

Everybody, everywhere
seeks happiness, it's true,
but finding it and keeping it
seems difficult to do.

Difficult because we think
that happiness is found
only in the places where
wealth and fame abound.

And so we go on searching
in palaces of pleasure
seeking recognition
and monetary treasure,
unaware that happiness
is just a state of mind
within the reach of everyone
who takes time to be kind.

For in making others happy
we will be happy, too,
for the happiness you give away
returns to shine on you.

He loves you!

It's amazing and incredible,
but it's true as it can be,
God loves and understands us all
and that means you and me -
His grace is all-sufficient
for both the young and old,
for the lonely and the timid,
for the brash and for the bold -
His love knows no exceptions,
so never feel excluded,
no matter who or what you are
your name has been included -
and no matter
what your past has been,
trust God to understand,
and no matter what your problem is
just place it in His hand -
for in all of our unloveliness
this great God loves us still,
He loved us since the world began
and what's more, He always will!

The richest gifts

The richest gifts
are God's to give
may you possess them
as long as you live,
may you walk with Him
and dwell in His love
as He sends you good gifts
from heaven above.

*It is by grace you have
been saved, through faith —
and this not from yourselves,
it is the gift of God.*

EPHESIANS 2:8

Other books
in this range

The Heart
of a Mother

Helen Steiner Rice™
Artwork by Cathi Freund

ISBN: 1-86920-357-7

ISBN: 1-86920-358-5

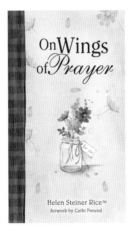

ISBN: 1-86920-359-3